Simulation Games
for Religious Education

by

Richard Reichert

JOHN KNOX PRESS
ATLANTA

Illustrations by
R.G. Davis

ISBN 0-8042-1436-0
Library of Congress Card Catalog Number 75-142

Contents

INTRODUCTION

Simulation Games in Education

Simulation as a teaching technique is basically *any* activity designed to produce a *feeling* similar to the feeling usually attached to a particular *life experience.* Let's take that definition apart. "Any" means that the term "simulation," as used here, is quite broad. It can be a very carefully researched and designed game, for example, such as the kind now produced commercially. Or it can be a simple party game, like a scavenger hunt, adapted for the teacher's purpose. *Feeling* is the key to all simulation games. In this context, feeling connotes generating an emotional state or combination of states. For example, the feeling a simulation game is designed to create may be one of frustration, fear, or loneliness in the initial part of the game followed by a feeling of relief at the end. Finally, "life experience" means any experience that can be found in real life which is presently beyond the student's normal experience or which he is not aware he is experiencing. A popular example involves feelings usually associated with prejudice. It is possible to simulate a situation in which students who normally don't experience being victims of prejudice obtain the feelings related to that experience.

So simulation is intended to produce particular feelings. The reason for producing such feelings is to supply a concrete experience out of which the teacher and students can enter into discussion and reflection upon the deeper issues related to the experience: the evil of prejudice, for example. It should be obvious that students who have just had a simulated experience of prejudice will be more receptive to and appreciative of comments regarding the real significance and effects of prejudice.

Simulation, therefore, is a means to an end, the end

being to help students gain a better insight into a particular truth, value, or evil related to faithlife.

As such simulation has several limitations. First, a simulation game will never be as effective as a real-life experience. A person simply can't fully experience what it is to be a victim of prejudice unless he is in fact a victim. Second, simulation is only one method for developing students' interest in and readiness for reflecting on a topic. There are other methods for achieving the same purpose, each with its own values and limitations. So simulation should be used selectively, not exclusively. Third, it must be kept in mind that a simulation game is only one part of a learning experience. Unless it is followed by some opportunity to reflect upon the real meaning behind the experience and by some opportunities to apply "the lesson" in real life, a simulation game becomes simply a time-filling activity—amusing perhaps but just a time-filler.

Simulation Games for Christian Concepts

These games were developed with a basic purpose in mind: to help teachers in religious education deal with some of the more difficult and abstract Christian concepts in experiential albeit simulated ways. What the games do for the teacher is provide interesting lead-ins for the topics, ones that hopefully catch students' curiosity and involve them immediately. After allowing the students to experience the topics and to find them pleasing, the teacher can initiate more technical or detailed discussions. Even so, once the students have gotten "into the topic," the teacher still must teach and the students still must come to grips with ideas and definitions. The games, then, provide a means for beginning this process.

The age group embraced by the games ranges from junior high students through adult. With appropriate adaptation, all the games can be used in both formal and informal settings. By their nature, though, most games are more effective in the flexible, informal settings like those found in CCD and retreat programs.

The topics covered are certainly not exhaustive. Rather they were selected with a view towards helping teachers present more difficult subjects. However, as the last chapter shows, there is a logical progression in the topics so that they can serve as a basis for several kinds of courses and programs.

Each game follows the same outline: Statement of Goal and Objective, Preparation and Materials Needed, Instructions, and Follow-up. The Goal is a statement of the immediate feeling or experience the teacher hopes to provide through the activity. The Objective is a statement of the larger purpose as it relates to one's overall faith-life and to the particular insights and convictions needed to live well. The Preparation section, as one might guess, states what the teacher must do before the session. The Instructions include both directions for the teacher and those to be offered to students. In every instance there are questions suggested to demonstrate how the teacher can move from the immediate experience of the game to the more theological or abstract ideas to be shared. The Follow-up is essential to the game. The questions suggested may not meet the teacher's needs entirely, but by all means some form of follow-up should be provided.

This brings us to an important point. Chapter 1 deals with the steps involved in developing simulation games. It is included for a special purpose. The hope is that by understanding what is involved in developing a game and by seeing a series of examples, the teacher will become interested in developing her or his own games. In other words, this set of games should be viewed as a jumping-off place by the teacher. One excellent reason for learning to develop simulation games is that they are not only effective educationally but are practical in terms of most religious education budgets. Usually the only cost is measured in terms of the teacher's willingness to spend time developing them.

As proof that one need not be an expert to develop his or her own games, it should be mentioned that several of those included here were developed by persons attending various workshops I have presented on the topic of gaming. In fact, some of the most effective games in the book were developed by "amateurs" after only a little practice. For example, take the game on page 28 called "Nonsense Syllables." It has been used with great success in a variety of settings. It was developed first by a group attending a workshop at the Espousal Center in Waltham, Massachusetts. They had no previous experience. This is not intended to give evidence to my capability as a teacher. Rather, it is proof that developing games is easier than most people seem to imagine.

Once a teacher has successfully developed a game or two, though, the temptation is to use games too frequently. As stated above, games are only one method, not the only method. If over-used they can become as stimulating as yesterday morning's oatmeal.

That reminds me of "The Oatmeal Game" on page 39. It is a good example of a game that might be adapted to meet different needs. Replace the oatmeal with water or milk to tone it down or substitute spaghetti to add more humor to the game. In a given situation it might be more effective to work with only a few volunteers rather than get the whole class involved. Or a teacher might decide that while the concept is good, it is impractical for her or his situation. That's when the teacher may want to develop a new game to achieve the same purpose.

Moreover, at no time should the teacher hesitate to adapt any of the games. Each game is a vehicle. Often the same game can serve many different purposes. The kinds of questions asked can make all the difference. For example, the "Authority/Obedience" game on page 82 is a variation of "Pin the Tail on the Donkey." It is used here in connection with certain problems of authority and obedience. In another instance, this game might stimulate a discussion on peer pressure, the nature of faith, the nature of trust, or even the helplessness and dependence experienced by one who is actually blind. What will make the difference are the kinds of follow-up questions asked by the teacher.

Finally, I have added as an appendix a reprint of an article I wrote on discussion techniques. Since one of the main purposes of gaming is to establish a climate for meaningful discussion and reflection, some of the tips included in the article will be useful. This is especially true if discussion is used as a follow-up session.

CHAPTER 1

DEVELOPING
SIMULATION GAMES

Of all the steps involved in developing a simulation game, none is more necessary and helpful than correctly defining your goal. Goal definition has two parts. First, it is necessary to refine the general topic of the lesson. For example, a general topic may deal with the Sacrament of Penance. It is necessary first to refine or narrow that topic to something more specific: the effect of sin and consequent effect of forgiveness, the communal dimension of the sacrament, or the purpose, value and history of auricular confession. While even such "specific" topics are still quite broad, at least they begin to give a more specific direction to the purpose of the lesson.

Assuming the general topic has been made sufficiently specific to be considered a goal for a lesson, it is now necessary to take a second step; that is, translate that goal into "feeling" terms. This is best done by asking a simple question: How can I provide the students with an experience of what it feels like to . . . ?

For example, using a topic mentioned above: the effect of sin and consequent effect of forgiveness, the question becomes: How can I provide students with an experience of what it feels like to be in sin and then experience forgiveness? At this point, it becomes a matter of trying to identify the kinds of feelings involved in the experience under question. Does the experience give one a feeling of pain, frustration, fear, isolation, anger? Is there a combination of feelings involved? What are these? Once you have identified at least some dominant feeling or feelings, the goal has been identified sufficiently to begin actually planning a simulation game. In our example, such a goal may read: To provide students with an experience of what it feels like to experience the isolation and helplessness associated with sinfulness and the consequent feeling of relief when a person is forgiven.

Having identified the feelings you need to produce, the task is to develop an experience that will produce such feelings. It is possible to identify certain elements that can be used to produce particular feelings. These become the building blocks for constructing a simulation game. Here is a list of some of the more important "feeling" producing elements used in constructing a game.

1) *Body positions:* Standing, kneeling, sitting, lying down—each of these positions will generate, at least in a low-key way, a particular feeling (power, vulnerability, being dominated, relaxed). If to this is added other options like placement of arms (overhead, behind back, crossed over chest, at the side, etc.), you can intensify a particular feeling.

2) *Senses:* Intensifying a particular sense experience will produce particular feelings; depriving a particular sense experience will produce others. For example, a brightly lighted room will create one mood or feeling, low lights will create another, and no lights will create a third. Music may be pleasing and create a feeling of peace, or it may be irritating if it is used as an obstacle to hearing something one wishes to hear. In this context, many simulations use such techniques as blindfolds or require silence for their performance or include music or some other source of sound to help create a particular feeling.

3) *Relationships and groupings:* Different feelings will be evoked by how participants are grouped. For example, if boys are formed into one group and girls into another, you set up a particular mood of safety or frustration, depending upon the age of the group. If you place one person in competition to a whole group you create another feeling. If you place persons "one on one" you create another. Such feelings will vary depending on the age of the group

and the nature of the activity. These relationships or groupings can be used to create a feeling of safety, fear, curiosity, competition, or isolation.

4) *Physical arrangement of persons:* This simply refers to how one arranges persons in the physical space available. For example, sitting in rows (typical classroom arrangement) creates one feeling. Sitting in circles creates another. Spreading persons as far apart as possible will have quite a different effect (isolation or safety) than having them hold hands while crowded closely together (intimacy).

5) *Physical arrangement of place:* This refers to the overall physical setting—the where and what of the place the activity is held. For example, an outside meeting is quite different from one in a small room. The kinds of decorations, lighting, various "props," or the absence of normal objects (chairs, for example) all produce certain feelings.

6) *Time:* The length or brevity of the activity will obviously have an influence on the feelings created. If it takes place within a short time limit, pressure, excitement, or frustration are some of the feelings that can be created. If the activity is designed to drag or if adequate time is provided, feelings like boredom can be produced on the one hand or, on the other, feelings of security and peace.

7) *Competition:* While a less tangible "element" than something like physical arrangement of place, competition has an obvious ability to produce certain feelings—fear, frustration, excitement, pride and a variety of subsequent feelings. Competition often involves several of the above mentioned elements: groupings (boys vs. girls, one vs. a group, group vs. group); time (brevity vs. length);

senses (non-verbal communication vs. ability to communi-
cate with words); body positions (some allowed a more
favorable position like being able to stand rather than
sit, etc.).

8) *Objects:* These can be categorized as valuable, curious, threatening, and functional.

a) valuable — asking a person for his watch to use in an
"experiment" will produce a different feeling than asking
a person for his handkerchief.

b) curious — a wrapped "mystery package" will produce
a certain interest; so will an automobile jack if produced
"out of context."

c) threatening — here we mean relatively threatening, as
opposed to actually threatening. A raw egg is a threatening object for a person wearing good clothes, if it is tossed
to him. Water is a typically threatening object to anyone
not dressed in a swimming suit. In this same category we
can introduce objects like paint, shaving lotion, and whip-
ping cream.

d) functional — in this category virtually anything can
be included if it serves the purpose of the game. Playing
cards, paper cups, cardboard boxes, crayons, paper bags —
anything useful to the design of the game.

This list of potential elements for producing certain
feelings is certainly not all-inclusive, but it is representa-
tive of elements used in constructing a simulation. Virtually all of these particular elements are within the control
of a religion teacher — and they don't involve much cost,
which is one of the values of a "homemade" simulation
game as a technique.

Having identified the feeling(s) you wish to produce
and possessing an awareness of some of the possible elements that can produce the feeling, the next task is to

construct some activity or game to serve as the framework for experiencing the feeling. For example, if your goal is to produce the feeling of isolation connected with sinfulness, you may wish to develop an activity in which certain participants become isolated from the rest of the group. You may intensify this feeling by adding other forms of isolation like depriving the persons of sight and forbidding them to speak. This feeling can be further intensified by having the participants sit down and form themselves into a tight ball by hugging their knees. Notice we use several elements to produce the feeling of isolation, but these elements must take place within some larger activity. The question then becomes: How do I get the participants to assume the postures that will produce the desired feelings?

While this raises the larger question of overall motivation, let's first deal with constructing the activity. Keep it simple! For example, ask the entire group to gather together into a close circle. Then ask that each person who has ever told a lie (even a little one) withdraw from the group as far as possible. Next ask that any person who has ever refused to share with another at any time in his life close his eyes. Finally, ask that all those who have ever been lazy and refused to do their share of the work at home sit down and form into a tight ball. All this can be done in silence. Assuming virtually everyone is now in some form of isolation from the rest of the group, let them all stay that way for perhaps a full minute. In using the element of time in a situation like this, a minute can seem like an hour and consequently heighten the overall experience. You can then reassemble the participants by saying that all those who have ever helped a stranger can resume a standing position, those who have ever sincerely apologized can open their eyes, etc., until all have been regathered into a tight circle.

A simple activity, but it provides a framework for introducing those elements which will produce feelings of isolation. It is not always easy to think up an activity — some people find this the hardest part of constructing a simulation — but it is really not so very difficult, and it becomes easier with practice. For starters, I suggest that a teacher become familiar with proven simulation games and begin to "hitchhike" from them; that is, develop variations to suit your needs. After a few successful efforts, the task of thinking up an activity or framework for creating the feelings becomes much easier.

The real task is to provide adequate motivation for the students to be willing to participate. In the example just given, it may be observed that there is no apparent motivation built into the exercise. In fact, two kinds of motivation could very easily be at work, inducing students to participate. The first is curiosity. Don't underestimate it. Students will often do quite bizarre things simply to find out "what's up." This presumes, however, that they have a basic trust of the teacher and haven't been tricked or manipulated by him in the past. The second motivation, confidence, is closely connected with the first and is based on past experience provided by the teacher which turned out to be fun and/or fruitful.

So students can be encouraged to participate because of curiosity. They can be motivated simply because past experience tells them that what the teacher is asking them to do will "go somewhere" no matter how strange it seems. A third kind of motivation is the spirit of competition or challenge built into an exercise. If it is introduced as something challenging, it will usually arouse interest — provided it is designed to avoid embarrassing individuals. (Normally it is all right to design an activity wherein one team loses, but it is not good in most instances to isolate one person as a loser.) Finally, some activities can be presented in such a way that they just sound like fun or provide a practical reward — and perhaps a change of pace from the usual routine of the class.

Assuming the teacher has identified the desired feelings to be produced, has designed an activity for producing them, and has provided adequate motivation, one step still remains in constructing simulation: the question/discussion phase.

Remember, the whole purpose of the simulation game is to provide the proper openness and opportunity for introducing reflection on a topic normally beyond the students' interest. The question phase has several parts. First, there are questions related to the immediate experience: How did you feel when . . . ? What was your immediate reaction as you . . . ? Were you very upset by . . . ?

Allow plenty of time for students to give their immediate reactions, including negative ones. The next kind of questioning should attempt to bridge from the immediate manufactured experience to more realistic experiences: Can you think of times in real life when you felt like that? Do you know of anyone who went through a real experience of isolation like that? Again, allow time for them to make the connection between the game and real life experiences, their own or those they have heard about.

Finally, the questioning should lead to making a connection between such life experiences and the topic behind your goal: Do you see any relation between this kind of experience and what a sinful person feels? Do you think sin produces that same kind of feeling of isolation? What is there about the nature of sin that could lead to feelings of isolation?

Note: Such questions, at least in general outline, should be carefully prepared ahead of time as part of the simulation game. In fact, some find it helpful to formulate the questions before they attempt to design the activity. It gives them a clearer idea of just where they want to go and what they want to achieve by the simulation. It's another way of defining the goal.

As mentioned above, the simulation game does not end here in terms of its purpose. If it succeeded and the initial round of questioning and discussion was successful, the teacher is now in a position to begin a more serious study of the topic. Interest has been aroused. There is a common concrete experience to which both students and teacher can refer. Whatever input follows can be related to something the whole class has experienced, at least in a simulated way.

Summary and Suggested Guidelines

As presented above, the process of constructing a simulation game involves these steps:

1) Refine the general topic to something manageable.

2) Define the topic in the form of a concrete goal: "The purpose of which is to produce an exercise of what it feels like to . . . "

3) Identify the particular feelings usually associated with the experience (anger, frustration, peace, fellowship, etc.).

4) Identify those elements or activities which can best produce the desired feelings (competition, groupings, sense deprivation, etc.).

5) Design an activity to serve as the framework for providing those elements. (Don't be afraid to borrow from proven simulations, party games, etc.).

6) As you design the activity, concern yourself with the basis for motivation: curiosity, challenge, fun, trust in

your past performance. (Combinations are likely.)

7) Prepare a list of questions to be used to stimulate discussion following the exercise. Questions can be divided into three phases: immediate reactions, relational questions, topic-oriented questions.

Some general guidelines for using simulations as a method in religious education may help the teacher avoid common pitfalls, most of which have been experienced by the author through a process of trial and error:

1) In most instances, don't bother to use them if you are teaching below the junior high level. You simply don't need them to produce the desired openness and interest in the topics you should be teaching.

2) On the junior high level, concentrate primarily on activities that center around competition rather than on those involving direct personal self-revelations. Also stress group rather than "one on one" competitions.

3) Never use a simulation when a real experience is available. For example, don't simulate an experience of the plight of the aged if it is possible to visit and serve persons in a nursing home.

4) Simulations that take place within the "real world" are more effective than those that take place in a classroom. For example, if you want to simulate what it feels like to be poor, it is better to send students out to try to panhandle the price of a decent meal than it is to play a game in the classroom.

5) Respect the emotional capacity of the participants. Don't create more frustration, self-disclosure or other feelings than they can handle. A good backup guideline is this: If you wouldn't do it, don't ask your students to do it.

6) Never manipulate the participants to the degree that they feel tricked or used. I grant that the whole concept of simulation implies a certain degree of surprise and/or

fabrication, but don't develop a simulation that ultimately results in resentment and distrust for the teacher. Simulation is a tool, not a weapon.

7) The final guideline is simply this: If by temperament you feel uncomfortable with the whole technique involved in simulation games, don't use them. Simulation is a good technique, but it isn't the only one.

CHAPTER 2

GAMES ON BASIC THEOLOGY

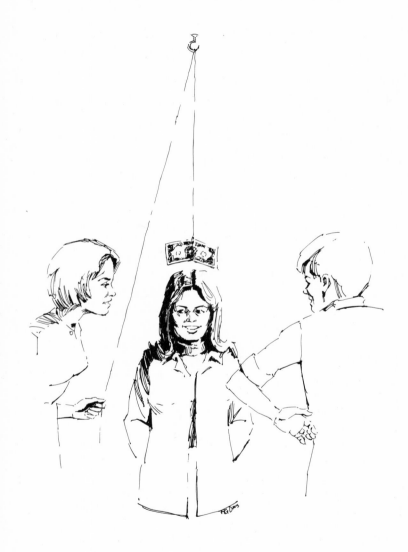

The Stretching Game

Goal

To give students a feeling of their personal limitations in a non-threatening way.

Objective

To introduce the students to the concept of man's limitations and dependence on God.

Preparation and Materials

You will need a long piece of string with a paper clip tied to one end. The string should be suspended from the ceiling in such a way that you can pull it up and down. Attach a dollar bill to the string with a paper clip.

Instructions

Introduce this exercise by commenting that some people believe it is possible to stretch the body as much as two inches using only concentration and muscle control. Not all people can do this. Just for fun, you would like to find out if any persons in the class have this capacity.

Then explain that you will suspend the dollar by the string slightly above the head of the participant (demonstrate). The participant must stand directly under the dollar, keep his feet flat on the floor (you may wish to appoint a "referee" to insure that this is done), place his hands behind his back and attempt, through stretching, to seize the dollar with his teeth. If he is successful he can keep the dollar.

Note: If you suspend the dollar to the point where it is just above the top of the person's head when he is standing *perfectly* straight he will be unable to reach it with his teeth. Yet he can come close enough to make it suspenseful.

After the explanation, give each person a chance to attempt the exercise. If you are working with a large group, you may wish to set up several strings so more than one person can try it at a time. Volunteers could help if necessary.

After each person has tried, or at least all who wish, reassemble the group and ask for some immediate reactions (frustration, doubt that it is possible, humor, embarrassment).

Then ask them to listen attentively to a short reading they have probably heard before, but which may now make a little more sense to them. Read Matt. 6:25-34.

Note: In this reading we are particularly interested in verse 27. In older translations it reads, "Which of you by worrying can add even one inch (cubit) to your height?" In newer translations it often reads, "Which of you . . . can add one minute to his lifespan." In your own reading, use the older translation above regardless of the text. The reason should be obvious. Also you will want to give special stress to that particular portion of the passage.

Next you will want to initiate discussion on the whole topic of man's limitations and his dependence on others and ultimately on "The Other." Some of the following questions may be helpful:

1) Is it significant that a man can't really add to his height? Is this symbolic of other more significant limi-

tations man experiences? What are some of the ways man is limited? Are there some kinds of limitations over which you have no control that tend to trouble you?

2) Where were you and what were you doing in 1950 (assuming no one in the group is older than twenty)? Where will you be and what will you be doing in 2075? Do you really have any control of that? What is the real meaning of the fact that your very existence is limited? Was there a time when you simply didn't exist as a person?

3) What about Jesus' advice concerning trusting in God? Is this a putdown, telling man that he is really very weak and must depend upon "Big Daddy" for help all the time? Or is it really very good advice?

4) Is there any relation between man's limitations and arguments for the existence of God? Does man's life really have any meaning if there is no "Other" who can overcome man's limits and give him perfection?

Follow-up

In another session or as a continuation of this one, you may wish to view and react to the film, *Late Great God* produced by the Paulist Fathers (Insight series).

In this same context, the students could read portions of *Jonathan Livingston Seagull* and react to the ideas presented about man's ideas and the idea of man's limitations and dependence upon God.

Or you may prefer to show one of many excellent films available dealing with astronomy as a means to evoke reflection on the power and wisdom of God in relation to Jesus' avowal of God's concern for man.

The Waiting Game

Goal

To give students an experience of some of the feelings involved in being hopeful.

Objective

To introduce students to the nature, basis, and qualities of Christian Hope.

Preparation and Materials

Note: Since this game requires a physical facility with several rooms to be used simultaneously or sufficient outdoor space to isolate several groups of students from each other, it probably won't be useful in a school setting. However, the game functions well in programs such as overnights, retreats, and the like. (An alternate adaptation for use in classrooms is found at the end of the game.) You will need a facility which allows you to separate several groups of students totally from each other.

Also prepare ahead of time the makings for a small party, including soft drinks, potato chips, cheeses, and the like. The party items can be as elaborate or as simple as you wish, but it is important that you conceal them from the students until the proper time. Finally, in each of the rooms or areas where you will "station" a group, place ahead of time materials that can be used to make party related objects. For example, in the first room place construction paper, scissors, and a stapler for making party hats. In the second, place a supply of poster paper and felt pens for making party posters. In the third, place a record player and piles of records from which the group should select some appropriate music for the party. In every room except one supply materials so that students become involved in a particular task as they wait.

Instructions

Begin the exercise by dividing the students into groups. The minimum size for a group should be four. The maximum size should be no larger than eight. The number of groups formed will depend on the number of students divided by the number of extra rooms or isolated areas you have available; for instance, twenty students and four rooms will divide into four groups of five. Once the groups are formed, ask the first group to come with you. Tell the others to remain in the main room until you return. Lead the first group to a room. Once there, tell them you are going to prepare a surprise party for the class. Ask them to help you by making hats and posters, selecting music, making fancy name tags, etc. Ask them to stay in the room until you return for them. *Don't tell them how long you will be.* Now return, get another group, and repeat the process until all the groups have been placed in different rooms. For the group that has no supplies, give them no further instructions except to wait. You will return when the party is ready.

Next do exactly as you promised. Set out the supplies. You can add an interesting dimension by returning to the main room and turning out all the lights, using another room for the actual party.

Now you must wait at least twenty minutes, letting enough time elapse so as to produce various reactions like impatience, suspicion, and the like. When you have decided enough time has elapsed, go to each group and if they are still there, ask them to bring what they have prepared to the party room. As you might suspect, there is a chance that a group will get tired of waiting and roam off. Often a group will send out a scout to see what's happening, so if they find the classroom dark, they'll relay this information. If you discover a scout, ask him to stay and help you. Don't let him return to tell the others. You may want to do some "spying" of your own during this time. If you're seen, just tell the students to be "patient." Once the group reassembles before the party begins, spend a few minutes getting immediate reactions from each group. Questions like the following should be sufficient:

1) Were you suspicious or did you believe me when I said I was going to prepare a party? Why? If you believed me at first, did you get suspicious as time went on?

2) What did your group do while you waited? Would you say the time went quickly, slowly? Do you think that as a group you used it well?

3) Did you send out a scout to find out what was going on? Why? (If he didn't come back: What did you think when he didn't return?)

After you have gotten an initial feel of the variety of their reactions, you can begin the party. However, it might be helpful to take a few quick notes to serve as a memory aid in the follow-up.

Follow-up

At your next meeting, or even during the party if students are sufficiently interested, comment on their reactions. What were the various ways persons and groups reacted when they were asked to "wait"? Some may have had positive experiences, some negative. A suspicious person might have injected suspicion into the group. Likewise, a trusting person may have found ways to support others and to help them wait. If some actually left the premises and missed the party, be sure to note this and ask for their comments. You will especially want to compare the reactions of the groups left with "something to do" and the group that was allowed simply to wait. When you feel the group has sufficient insight into the variety of ways people react to waiting, begin to relate this to the situation of the Christian. Briefly this means recalling how Jesus asked us to wait while he prepared a "party" for us. He promised he would come back for us, but he did not say just when that would be. Meanwhile, he asked us to help in the preparations, that is, to work creatively to build the spirit of love (the party spirit) by caring for and working with each other.

Note: Theologically the analogy obviously limps, but the actual refinements regarding the nature of hope and the mission of Christians in the world can be developed once you make the initial tie-in between this exercise and the concept of Christian hope. You can further observe how various people react differently to Jesus' promise. We're still waiting. Some are confident and busy, working to prepare all men for the party. Others are suspicious. Still others no longer believe in Jesus' promise and are still trying to figure out what we're doing here. The real point, of course, is that to be a Christian is to learn to believe in Jesus' promise and to learn how to help prepare all men for the party. Just as waiting isn't always easy, so hope is not easy. But armed with confidence in Jesus' promise, the Christian can afford to work courageously for his fellow man, convinced that, in the end, his efforts will have been worthwhile no matter how bad things do look at various points in history.

Alternate Exercise: When it is impossible to send students to various rooms, one possibility is for the teacher to leave. Follow instructions as above and then leave the room. All groups work in the same room. Remain away long enough to evoke some suspicion or impatience. When you do return be sure to have some kind of surprise, even if it is no more than a candy bar for each person. Follow up with the same pattern of questions as above, adapting as necessary to fit your situation.

Nonsense Syllable

Goal

To give students a feeling of moving from chaos to unity through the insight of a "prophet" who discerns their spirit.

Objective

To introduce them to the topic of the Spirit's presence and work among them and to the role of the prophets in our community.

Preparation and Materials

Prepare as many sets of "three by five" cards as needed, one set to each group of six in your class. (For instance, twenty-four students require four sets). Each set will contain five cards. One syllable will be printed on each card as follows:

    card one _____CUM
    card two _____ HO
    card three _____LEE
    card four _____SPEAR
    card five _____ IT

If each syllable is said in that sequence, we obviously have the expression, "Come, Holy Spirit." Shuffle each set of cards.

Instructions

Form groups of six. Designate one person in each group as a leader. Explain to all groups the following rules:

1) Each person in a group will be given a card with a syllable on it.

2) At a signal all persons in the group are to begin to say loudly their syllable—in a monotone. Demonstrate what is meant by a monotone. Continue to repeat this syllable over and over loudly.

3) The leader's task is to listen to each sound, rearrange persons in the order he thinks they should be, and then have them express their sound *in turn*. If done properly the result will turn from noise to meaningful expression.

Assign groups to various parts of the room. Proximity adds to the confusion, competition, and fun of the exercise. Give the signal to begin. Allow the activity to continue until all groups have finally succeeded. This will happen quickly once the first group is heard.

Reassemble the class and seek reactions, using some of the following questions:

1) Besides amusement, what were some of your feelings when the exercise began? Frustration? Confusion? Helplessness? Curiosity? (Be sure to ask leaders how they felt too.)

2) How did those feelings contrast with the feelings you had as things began to get in order? As you began to see what it was all about? Why?

3) Did you begin to feel a sense of "togetherness" and purpose once you were doing it right? Why? Why not?

4) Did this experience recall to you any real life situations in which, although everything began in a confused way, order and meaning began to emerge? When? What? Who was involved? Who put the order into the operation?

5) Do you think in real life each person has a special gift, a talent, or a task? Do you think if someone could recognize these and get us working together we'd all be better off? Is that what it means to be a leader—to see how people can best work together without destroying the unique contributions of each individual?

Follow-up

At an appropriate point (or in another session) the teacher will want to speak about the relationship between the exercise and the Christian beliefs about the role of the Spirit and the role of the prophet:

1) The Spirit gives unique gifts to each person.

2) These gifts could go unrecognized and unused if we don't have prophets: persons whose special gift is the capacity to recognize the presence or absence of the Spirit and to tell others about it.

3) The end result—if we listen to the prophets and cooperate with the Spirit—is a growing together as community. Each person remains unique, but we all work together. A new reality emerges.

Note: We are stressing the positive effect of the presence of the Spirit and the role of the prophet as leader or catalyst for forming community. There is also the negative dimension. When the Spirit is absent, there is no community. In this case the prophet's role is to discern and proclaim this absence, an absence that is filled by some form of evil (spirit). So the role of the prophet will often involve challenging people, confronting them with the evil they are embracing. More often than not, this is the common understanding of the prophet (aside from predicting the future). He is seen as social revolutionary. In fact, the gift of prophecy is basically the gift of discerning the Spirit *and* his absence. It goes both ways. In either case, his task is to proclaim what he sees. This can be dangerous. If he succeeds and the people respond, the result is always community.

Each Man's Music

Goal

To give students an experience in "discerning the
spirit."

Objective

To continue discussion on the role of the Spirit in their
lives and in the lives of others.

Preparation and Materials

You will need recordings of three or four diverse kinds
of music (classical, rock, country/western). Exclude
vocals. It might be simpler if you pre-recorded short
selections of each kind of music onto a tape or a cassette.

You will also need a recording of some famous speech,
such as Martin Luther King's "I Have a Dream." You will
want a selection that has some moving, emotional quality to it. This selection could also be pre-recorded onto
the same tape.

Finally, choose one of Jesus' discourses from the Gospels,
such as his presentation of the Beatitudes or part of his
Last Supper conversation. If you prefer have someone
with skill in dramatic reading pre-record the selection.

Instructions

Begin by asking the class to listen to several different
kinds of music you have prepared for them. Play each

selection in turn, pausing a moment or so between the different kinds. It is best if the selections are played in some kind of sequence, for instance, hard rock to classical.

After all selections have been played, ask students several of the following questions:

1) Can you describe the different moods each music created in you? Peaceful? Exciting? Happy? Sad?

2) Were there any physical effects, such as foot tapping?

3) If we were to say each selection had a different kind of spirit to it, could you label each? For example, the first selection contained a spirit of excitement, the second a spirit of . . . (It is not necessary for the whole class to arrive at a consensus for each label. The main effort is to get the students thinking in terms of music "containing and being able to pass on" a kind of spirit. Once they have caught the idea, ask them to listen to your recording of the famous speech. A section from it may be sufficient. Now using some of the following questions continue the discussion:)

4) Could you say the man speaking was also playing a kind of music, a music that created a mood or a spirit in you? What was that mood or spirit? Did it affect you in other ways?

5) Do you think it's safe to say that each person in his own way plays a kind of music by his words and deeds, by his presence? That each person contains a kind of spirit and passes this on by his words and actions, possibly affecting others with it?

6) Can you think of any persons you met who did or do

this for you? Like a coach, a teacher, a friend? What kind of spirit do they radiate?

Once the students have begun to think of each person possessing and radiating a particular mood or spirit, ask them to listen to the last selection, the reading from the Gospel. Continue by asking similar questions, but make sure you ask them to try to give words or descriptions to the spirit radiated by Jesus (peace, strength, kindness, courage).

Next, explain that Jesus' spirit is the Spirit of God. We can best recognize when the Spirit of God is present or absent by the kinds of effects he causes: peace, courage, gentleness, strength. You will want to mention that to be a Christian means that a person consciously and willingly allows Jesus' Spirit to take hold of him, to live in him. In other words, a Christian is one who lives by the Spirit of Jesus and radiates that same spirit to others. Obviously each person does this in a different way and to a different degree.

Follow-up
In the same session or in the next one, you will want to pursue the topic further with questions like the following:

1) What's involved in catching the spirit of someone and in particular Jesus (openness, contact, listening, *prayer*)?

2) In this context how would you best describe prayer? How necessary does it become for anyone trying to live by the Spirit of Jesus?

3) Finally, at this moment in your life how would you

best describe the "music" you play, the spirit you radiate to others? What spirit do you live by? Are you happy with it?

This last question is crucial. It opens the door for some serious self-reflection. If the group is not sufficiently mature, you may not want them to share their reflection with others, but at least have them think about it. In groups that have sufficient rapport, you could divide into smaller groups and let each one give the other some feedback, that is, share with one another what kind of spirit each person seems to radiate.

Conclude by commenting that a person who has a special skill in "hearing the music of the Spirit" wherever it is played is a prophet. This will lead into the next game.

Our Town

Goal

To give students an opportunity to attempt to do some "discerning of the Spirit" in various situations.

Objective

To help them form a deeper insight into prophetic role of the Christian in society and the problems one can expect to find in fulfilling that role.

Preparation

The two previous activities are the best preparation for this one. No special materials are needed.

Instructions

After concluding the two previous activities, give the students this "take home" assignment: (If possible conduct a "field trip," and then have the students return for this discussion).

1) Between now and the next meeting attempt to discern the kind of spirit that seems to dominate in at least three of the following possible places:

    a) your own home
    b) the school cafeteria
    c) some place where youth gather regularly
    d) a bus station or similar place
    e) the congregation at a typical Sunday Mass

f) a party or dance you attend
g) a busy downtown street

2) In trying to discern the "music" or spirit of the place, ask yourself these questions:
   a) do you experience any dominant mood or feeling?
   b) can you give it a name?
   c) would you say it is basically in agreement with or in contradiction to what you consider to be the Spirit of Jesus? In other words, is the Spirit of Jesus present or absent?
   d) if the situation seems to have several kinds of "spirit" involved, which tends to dominate, the Spirit of Jesus or one contradictory to Jesus?

Tell the students you would like them to report on their experiences when you meet again.

Follow-up

At the next session or after the "field trip," ask them to share their findings. This will give you a good idea about how much sensitivity they are developing in terms of being in tune with themselves and with the Spirit.

Allow sufficient time for this discussion. Then, assuming some students judged that signs of Christ's Spirit were totally or significantly lacking in some situations, ask them these questions:

1) We've said that a prophet is one who points out to others when the Spirit of Christ is present or absent. Given the situation mentioned by (a particular student), how would you even begin to be prophetic in that situation? What could you say? How might you act to make your point?

2) What kind of response might you expect from the people involved?

3) Would this be a pretty risky situation? What would be necessary for you personally to be willing to take that kind of risk?

In this way you can lead them into discussion and make observations about the role of the Christian in society. In this context you can draw upon examples of Old Testament prophets, of the life of Jesus, and of some persons you might judge to be contemporary prophets. Make the distinction between such special prophetic vocations and the common vocation of all Christians to act prophetically in their every day situations. Stress also how a faith community working together can have a prophetic effect on society through its actions or witness.

D. SIN AND THE NATURE OF MAN

The Oatmeal Game

Goal

To give students an experience of what it feels like to contradict their "nature."

Objective

To introduce them to some concepts about the nature of sin.

Note: The key behind this exercise is the teacher's understanding that morality—here limited to mean one's experience of personal guilt or holiness (wholeness)—is dependent upon a person's self-understanding. If a person accurately understands "who he is" and knowingly acts contrary to that conviction, he is apt to feel uneasy. (Conscience is that sensitive awareness that a certain behavior is not consistent with a particular conviction about oneself.) A false understanding of oneself, regardless of how it is acquired, is equivalent to a "false conscience." For example, a youth who is told he is lazy will act lazily and not feel bad about it. The Christian is graced with God's revelation of who a person really is: son or daughter of the Father, sister or brother to all men, heir to the Father's kingdom. A Christian is one who understands his "nature" in the light of this revelation and acts accordingly. To act contrary to this awareness is to become involved in sinfulness, to become inhuman.

Preparation and Materials

You will need a box of instant oatmeal, a large mixing

39

bowl and some saucers, access to hot water for preparing the oatmeal. Some towels for cleaning up will also be needed.

Instructions

Divide the class into groups of six; explain that each group will be involved in a kind of contest. While it may seem foolish to them, it's important that each one cooperate since there is a rather serious purpose behind the contest.
The rules are simple:

1) Each group will be provided with one saucer of warm oatmeal.

2) The group is to kneel in a small circle around it.

3) At the signal each person in the group is to take a turn at trying to lap up some oatmeal, keeping hands behind the back, repeating the process until one group "cleans" their saucer. That group is the winner.

Proceed to have them kneel in position and present each group with its saucer. (You can anticipate that some won't cooperate, but it makes no difference for the success of the exercise.) After one group has in fact cleaned its saucer or at least given it a try, call an end to the exercise and give the students a chance to clean up. Next reassemble them and initiate discussion with some of the following questions:

1) How did you feel when I suggested the activity? Why? (In case some did not participate at all, ask why they resisted. Some may answer that they would feel like animals or that it was "gross" or "unnatural" to eat like that.)

2) How did you learn that eating like that isn't right? Who taught you? How long have you known that's not the way to eat? Do you feel most men throughout the civilized world would react pretty much the same way?

3) Can you think of any other things you have done in which you felt you were going against the grain?

4) Do you think you might have something of the same kind of feeling if you were asked to do something extremely unnatural, like murdering another human being? What other kinds of actions might give you something of that same feeling? Why?

Having moved the topic more directly into the realm of morality, the teacher will want to show that sin is essentially acting contrary to our awareness of who we really are. In this context, this self-awareness can be called conscience. Our conscience or self-awareness can be incomplete or inaccurate if we don't have an adequate awareness of what it really means to be fully human. Christians believe that through Jesus we understand what it really means to be human. The understanding of that revelation forms the basis of a Christian conscience. For a Christian to act contrary to that awareness is to act contrary to what is most authentic in him. In a sense, at least, the Christian who sins will experience something of the repugnance you experienced in eating the oatmeal.

Having developed this theme the teacher will want to apply these principles in later sessions to particular moral issues, relating them to Christ's revelation about who man really is.

Follow-up

Using the ten commandments, ask students to review in groups of six to eight whether or not what is forbidden is "being inhuman." Or you may wish to assign one commandment to several groups for the same discussion and then compare results.

CHAPTER 3

GAMES ON COMMUNITY

The Balloon Game

Goal

To give students an experience of the feeling of cooperation and the results of non-cooperation.

Objective

To introduce them to one aspect of what it means to be a community.

Preparation and Materials

After dividing the class into groups of six to eight persons, you will need one balloon for each group. With a felt-tip pen write the words "Good News" on each balloon. Arrange the room so that a group can move *as a group* from one end to the other.

Instructions

Explain to the groups that you are conducting an experiment in cooperation. Ask one group to volunteer to be first. Have them form in a tight circle at one end of the room. Explain that their task is to try to move from one end of the room to the other without breaking the circle and while keeping the balloon afloat in their midst. Everyone in the group is to participate. Time them until they make it to the other end (usually there is no trouble). If the balloon falls they are to return to the starting place and begin over. Each group receives a turn and whoever makes the best time is the winner.

Next, explain that the same procedure is to be repeated,

but this time only half the group may help keep the balloon in the air. Designate the non-participants. These non-participants are to remain in the group and move along with it, but they must keep both hands behind them. If time permits you could repeat the exercise a third time, allowing only two from each group to use their hands. In this case, make sure the two are on opposite sides of the circle.

After the activity, reassemble the class and use some of the following questions to stimulate reactions:

1) How did you feel toward the others when all were cooperating? Closeness? Certain confidence that you could do it? A kind of spirit of togetherness?

2) How did you feel toward the members of your group when they weren't participating? How did you feel as a group? Did you lose some of your closeness or spirit? Would it have been easier if they had dropped out altogether? Were they just in the way?

3) If you were one of those who had to put his hands behind his back, what was your reaction? helplessness? frustration? indifference toward the task? Did you still feel you were part of the group? Did you feel the others resented you?

4) Can you think of any real situations where you were part of a task group in which some did not participate (for instance, your family, a team, a club or a job)? How did you feel? Did they hinder the group?

5) Can you think of situations when you were part of a group but for some reason were not allowed to participate in its task? How did you feel? Why?

6) Can we say that the ideal situation for a group or "community" is one in which everyone is allowed to participate in its task and in which everyone assumes her or his responsibility to do so?

This should allow the teacher to turn naturally to a discussion of the Church as a community. How well do people cooperate in the common task? What is the common task of the Church as a community? Is it to keep the faith alive as it proceeds through history? Who have "their hands behind their backs"? Why? Do the students feel persons their age participate in the Church's common task? Why? Why not? Should they? What could or should they do in terms of participation?

Follow-up

The best kind of follow-up would be for the group to plan and execute a short-term project where all have some clear responsibilities (for example, planning a surprise party for another class). Then have them analyze the results of the project. Did they function as a community? Did they grow together as a community? Why or why not?

Pizza Scavenger Hunt

Goal

To give students an experience of celebrating a shared success.

Objective

To introduce a discussion on the nature of the Church as a Eucharistic community.

Preparation and Materials

This game can be very effective, but because it requires access to a kitchen and to some cooking utensils, it is designed primarily for programs held in a person's home or in an overnight retreat setting. However, a variation can be used in situations where no kitchen is available. This will be explained later. What is needed are the facilities and utensils necessary for making a pizza (more than one if the group is large). While it is not absolutely necessary, it might be wise to have available (unknown to the students) at least the basic ingredients for a pizza: flour, tomato paste and cheese.

Instructions

Present the class with a "shopping list" of ingredients for having a pizza party. A sample list would include:

1) flour (enough to accommodate the group)
2) tomato paste
3) cheese
4) sausage

5) olives
6) mushrooms
7) (other ingredients)
8) kool aid mix or other beverage

The list can be as simple or complex as you think appropriate. Having presented the list, explain that within a given time limit (depending on how much meeting time is available) they are to attempt to scavenge the ingredients listed and return to the meeting place. A pizza(s) will be made from whatever ingredients are acquired. (Hence it is a good idea to have the essentials on hand as a backup.) The only rules are: don't steal and don't buy the ingredients. At this point, divide the class into an appropriate number of groups, one group for each ingredient needed. If you end up with more than three to a group, it is better to divide the class in half first, each half being responsible for getting the same ingredients. Ask each group to volunteer to get one item until all items are covered.

Remind them of the time limit and send them out. As the groups return, gather their materials. When all have returned, take stock of what you have and if necessary provide any basics that are missing. Ask for some volunteers to make the pizza(s). While this is taking place, assemble the others and initiate a discussion with some of the following questions (after allowing time first for the groups to share any adventures they experienced on their outing):

1) If you succeeded in getting your item, what was your immediate feeling or reaction?

2) If you were unable to get your item, how did you feel about returning to the others?

3) If you were successful in getting your item, how did you feel toward others who were not successful (if this happened)? Why?

4) Do you think regardless of how they taste the pizzas we will share will have a special quality? That they will kind of bring us closer together? Why?

5) When something that is acquired through common effort is shared, does it produce a certain sense of celebration? Why?

6) Can you think of any other experiences where a group you were in cooperated in doing and then sharing something? What? Was it a kind of celebration? Why?

7) Can you see any kind of relationship between what we did tonight and what the Church does when it celebrates the Eucharist?

Once you have moved the discussion to this point, don't hesitate to add your own comments about the nature of Eucharistic community whenever appropriate: how all are responsible for bringing something of themselves to the group, how in this coming together we produce a very special bread, the Bread of life, how in sharing this bread we celebrate our brotherhood and our hope for our future, and how this celebration can be weakened when some don't share of themselves. As much as possible, though, try to elicit such observations from the students themselves.

Once the pizza is ready, you can have your party. However, you may wish to solemnize it a bit first by having an appropriate reading like Acts 2:43-47 or 1 Cor. 11:17-26.

Follow-up

The logical follow-up is the preparation for, planning, and celebrating an actual Eucharist together, following somewhat the same procedure wherein various groups are responsible for providing elements: music, altar bread, wine, decorations, readings. (No scavenger hunt, though).

Variation of the Above: Where time and/or facilities make it impossible to have a pizza scavenger, follow the same procedure as above substituting for pizza ingredients the ingredients for a hero sandwich or a variety of snacks that need no special preparation:

Hero Sandwiches	*Party Snacks*
French bread or buns	potato chips
cold cuts	a dip or two
cheese	crackers
lettuce	cheeses
pickles	pretzels
mustard, butter, mayonnaise	beverage
tomatoes	
beverage	

C. COMMUNITY, FREEDOM AND AUTHORITY

Senses Walk

Goal

To give students an experience of the feelings and conflicts involved in trying to achieve a common goal without taking away the freedom of individuals.

Objective

To introduce a discussion on the need for authority, freedom, and obedience within the community.

Preparation and Materials

No special materials or preparation are necessary for this exercise. However, you will want to determine a starting point and finishing point appropriate for the time and facilities available. This will become clear after you read the instructions for the activity.

Instructions

The class must be divided into groups of six. If this doesn't come out even, extra students should join the existing groups. Designate one person in each group to be a particular sense, another person in each group to be another sense until all the five senses are represented: sight, taste, touch, smell, and hearing. The sixth person in each group is designated intellect/will. Extra persons in a group are identified as any of the five senses and should team up with the other person who is that sense.

Now explain the rules of the activity as follows:

1) Each group is to take a "walk" from this room to (designate a location) and back again.

2) Each "sense" is allowed and encouraged to seek out anything appropriate to his nature, for example, "sight" should seek out pleasant objects to view; "touch" should explore tactile experiences of smooth, rough, soft, hard. The more that each sense experiences the better.

3) However, each group should be back within 5-10 minutes. (Five minutes is usually sufficient; anything beyond ten minutes usually destroys the effect.)

4) Intellect/will is responsible for getting the entire group back on time. Therefore, each sense *must* obey intellect/will when he or she says to move on. At the same time the intellect/will should try to allow each "sense" maximum freedom within that time limit, that is, allow them to wander and pursue as many experiences as possible.

5) Only intellect/will can talk.

Once everyone understands the rules, signal for each group to begin its walk.

When all have returned, initiate discussion with some of the following questions:

1) To the "senses": What are some of the things you experienced? Did any particular object turn you on more than others? Did you find it difficult trying to be only one sense? Did you discover things you normally don't notice?

2) To the "senses": How did you react to intellect/will

when he ordered you to move on? Did you resent him? Did you find it easy? Did you wish you could have stayed, when you knew it was best to move on?

3) To the "senses": How did you feel toward the other senses? Did you notice what they were doing? Did you feel a comradeship or any sense of responsibility to co-operate? A sense of competition?

4) To the leaders: How did you feel in your task? Why? Did the members cooperate? Did you find it difficult to try to give each sense maximum freedom and still keep the group moving in the right direction within the time limit? Did you start out by being lenient and gradually become more demanding? Or did you do the reverse? Why did you change if you did?

5) To the group which returns first: Did you feel you were pressured by intellect/will or did you feel you were given sufficient freedom?

6) Direct the same questions to the other groups, especially to the group last in returning.

7) Can you think of real life situations of a similar kind? What were these? How did you feel and act in these situations?

8) Is there any "truth" involved here in regard to how a real community functions? Freedom and obedience? Personal uniqueness and cooperation? The need for some kind of authority? Can you think of examples?

9) Since we regard the Church as a community, what kind of application can we make here in regard to authority/obedience/personal freedom within the Church?

Having reached this point in the discussion, the teacher should be ready to make more direct contributions about the need for authority and obedience and the obvious difficulties involved in trying to reach particular goals while preserving individual freedom. Stress should be placed on the fact that a person necessarily doesn't lose his freedom or uniqueness by following orders to achieve a common purpose.

Follow-up

Identify one particular problem the students experience in relation to Church authority, for instance, mandatory Mass attendance on Sundays. Examine this issue in terms of individual freedom, the need for cooperation, the difficulty of authority in keeping the group functioning together.

Note: This exercise has many uses with appropriate changes in questions and follow-up. For example, it has application to the personal experience of students trying to get themselves together, that is, finding a balance between allowing a healthy freedom to their senses and maintaining an integrity that allows for purposeful action. It could have application to family life in that the father and mother could be equated to intellect/will while the children are at least in one aspect like the individual senses needing guidance and direction. In short, any authority/obedience situation could be explored by the use of this exercise.

If the teacher fears this kind of exercise creates an inaccurate split between intellect-will-senses in the minds of students, he or she may wish to explain that these divisions are rather artificial, but are useful for the purposes of the game. Normally, however, students are more interested in the game and don't become involved in the philosophical and psychological implications.

Go Away, Come Back

Goal

To give students an experience of rejecting and then forgiving a disruptive member.

Objective

To initiate discussion on the effect of sin and reconciliation within the Christian community.

Preparation and Materials

For the exercise you will need a supply of toothpicks, a household glue, and posterboard for each group of six to eight. You may want to provide additional supplies such as scissors, string, felt pens, and the like.

Instructions

Divide the class into groups of six to eight. Using the supplies provided, each group is to work together to design and then construct a symbol of what "community" means to them. It may be as elaborate or simple as they wish. A time limit should be set. Students are advised that each group should be prepared to explain their symbol once it is finished.

Before the class begins, however, select one student in each group and instruct him or her to act as an obstructionist. Tell the student to argue, refuse to cooperate, hinder progress, and the like. Try not to make the behavior too obvious, though. The purpose, it should be explained to them, is to test out the group's reaction to such behavior. With such a "plant" in each group, tell the students to begin their project. After they have been involved long enough so that the "plant" in each group has aroused sufficient aggravation, call a temporary halt to the activity.

Explain, that for purposes of experiment, you would like to form a new group by obtaining one member from each existing group, to see if the new group could "catch up" with the others. Advise each group to reject one person from their membership who will then form the new group. Normally, each group will reject the troublemaker, but even if another is rejected, it does not alter the exercise. Let the groups proceed while you meet with the outcasts. Explain that in a minute or two each is to return to his original group and ask to be readmitted, saying they don't like the new group. Tell them to observe the reactions of various members carefully. Send the outcasts back to their groups. You should observe the reactions carefully too.

When each group has had sufficient time to react, either by accepting a person back or by refusing readmittance, stop the activity and call all the groups back together. Initiate discussion with some of the following questions: (It is good to explain each group had a plant.)

1) Why did you reject the person you did?

2) How did you feel about having to reject him?

3) How did you feel when he returned and asked to be readmitted? Why?

4) If you refused to reaccept him, what was your reason?

5) If you accepted him back, why? Did you place any conditions for accepting him back?

6) How did you show him you really accepted him back? Why did you say or do what you did?

7) To the "plants": How did you feel about the whole process?

Once their initial reactions have occurred, direct the discussion more into questions of religious significance:

1) Moral theologians observe that sin involves to some degree a disruption of community. By his actions, the sinner isolates himself from the community. In the light of what we have been doing, does this make sense? Why?

2) In the same way, reconciliation is said to involve being readmitted into the community. Is this a good way to view it? Why? Why not?

3) For reconciliation to happen, the sinner must show some signs of his sincerity and the community must indicate that they do accept him back. Was any of that happening here?

4) Can you think of any real instances where you were involved in a group in which a person was rejected and then readmitted? Why was he rejected? In what way was he readmitted? What "signs" were involved? Handshakes? Formal apologies? Words of acceptance?

5) Can you see how any of this relates to Church, sin and the sacrament of reconciliation? What's involved when a person who is "outside the community," that is, in sin, seeks readmittance?

By this time the whole conversation can move more directly to a discussion of the nature of sin and the sacrament of reconciliation. You should not hesitate to take a more active part at this time, showing how the Church expects some signs of repentance on the part of the sinner and, also, how important it is for the Church to give real signs that they do welcome back the individual.

Follow-up

An ideal follow-up would be for the class to plan and then participate in some form of communal penance service.

CHAPTER 4

GAMES ON THE NATURE OF PRAYER

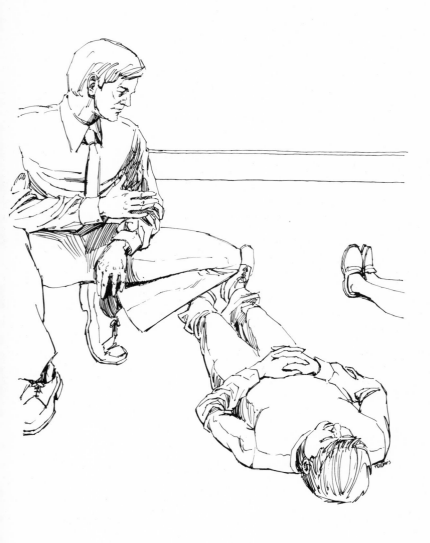

A. AN EXPERIENCE OF PRAYER

Spirit Walk

Goal

To give students an actual experience of what is involved in meditation as a technique for prayer.

Objective

To assist them in understanding and to stimulate in them the practice of meditation on a regular basis.

Preparation and Materials

While the exercise can be done virtually anywhere if students are properly motivated, a quiet comfortable atmosphere makes it more effective. So if possible prepare the room with soft light and perhaps some low, soothing instrumental music. If the room is carpeted you should have the students lie on the floor. All outside noises and distraction should be avoided as much as possible.

Instructions

Tell students you are going to take them on an imaginary walk. Instruct them to get as comfortable as they can and close their eyes.

Note: Some will open eyes several times to "check" things out. Call them by name and ask them in cordial terms to keep their eyes closed. Explain that no trick is involved and that it is essential that they get completely relaxed, which includes closing the eyes. In a quiet voice tell them to continue to relax and explain:

"We are going on a spirit journey. We are going to free our spirit from our body first." Begin using phrases like the following:

"Your spirit is now leaving your feet and legs. They are now totally asleep . . . .

"Your spirit is now going up through your stomach and chest . . . out of your arms . . . up through your neck . . . now out the top of your head . . . ."

Note: there may be a few giggles initially, but keep going. Individuals will settle down.

"Your spirit is now out of your body . . . look down at your body lying there . . . you are temporarily freed from its weight, from feeling, from any pains it has. We will come back to it shortly, but for now let's enjoy the freedom we have as spirits . . . .

"Wander about the room, weightless and free . . . Now let's go out the door . . . down the corridor . . . past the (some reference point) . . . out the (front) door . . . ."

Note: always speak in a low voice, steady and soothing, pausing after your phrasings sufficiently for them to imagine what you are suggesting.

"Now that you are free, travel to your favorite place, regardless of what part of the world it is, the place you most enjoy when you are alone . . . . "See it . . . notice everything present . . . sun or stars . . . trees or water, all the sights and smells and sounds of your favorite place . . . relax there and enjoy it . . . Think of some person with whom you would like to share your innermost thoughts. Imagine that this person is right there beside

you . . . looking at you . . . waiting for you to say something . . . . *Tell him or her now whatever it is you most
want to say . . . . Ask for whatever you most desire . . . .
Let the person answer you . . . . What does he or she say
to you? What is being asked?*

"Your friend leaves . . . . It's time to go back to your
body . . . away from your favorite place . . . back outside this building . . . through the (front) door . . . (continue this return, covering each identical area you observed on your journey until each has returned to his own
body—right down to his feet.)"

Now tell students to open their eyes and get up. They
can move around and talk.

After a few minutes reassemble and explain that they
have just meditated in the best sense of the term. Analyze
for them the key elements of this form of meditation:
relaxation, concentration that eliminates distraction, the
focus of one's attention on a loved person and then a
heart-to-heart, honest conversation with him or her in
one's own words. While this kind of meditating is best
done in a quiet spot like a room or a chapel or some pleasant place out of doors, it can be practiced virtually anywhere if students are willing to work at the concentration
involved. It isn't necessary to go through all the mechanics of "leaving your body." This is a kind of gimmick
that is helpful to some to focus their attention, but all
kinds of other means can be used. Use the spirit journey
only if it seems helpful.

Note: don't elicit student observations on what happened to them during the exercise. These should be left
as private, personal experiences. However, at this point,
you may wish to get reactions to the idea of meditation in
general and this form of meditation in particular.

Follow-up

As a kind of assignment, ask each student to try at least once before the next session to meditate in the way you have been describing. Choose a time and place, relax, concentrate, taking the spirit walk if it helps to insure a sense of peace and recollection. At the next meeting at least some time should be spent asking students to talk about how things went. You are not interested in the "content" of the exercise, but rather in any success or difficulties they experienced in concentrating, how real or phoney it felt, if they think this is in fact a true form of meditating.

One Word of Caution: Since the exercise uses some of the techniques involved in hypnosis, it may have a stronger effect on a very sensitive person. For that reason the teacher should always be careful to "bring them back" the same way they went out. The risk of the exercise having an actual hypnotic effect is slight unless a person has a serious emotional disturbance. This teacher has never experienced any bad effects in students when using this exercise.

What Did He Say?

Goal

To give students an experience of various forms and levels of listening.

Objective

To illustrate that aspect of prayer/dialogue called listening.

Preparation and Materials

For this exercise you will need a record player and a recording of a popular hymn. Recommended is Joe Wise's "Hear Me," but some similar song of your choice will work well. Also have ready papers and pencils, a copy of the New Testament or at least a copy of the parable of the Prodigal Son. Finally, you will need enough apples and/or oranges (grapes, leaves, rocks or any natural object can be used as a substitute) so that each student can receive one.

Instructions

Introduce the exercise by saying it is a test in their listening ability. Explain that you are going to play a familiar song. With the paper and pencils provided they are to keep track of the number of times the word "the" occurs in the song. (If you want to complicate it a little give them two words to listen for.) The purpose is to find out how many can come up with the exact number.

Play the song. Tell them to write down the results of

listening. Play it a second time, giving them a chance to double check. After the second playing, ask them to put their final answer down. Ask for results. Compare these with the exact number (which you determined by having listened previously and/or by having checked against a written copy of the song). Comment appropriately on how many were correct, incorrect, how many changed answers from the first to second listening, and so on.

Now explain you want to test them on their ability to listen on another level. While listening to the same song, ask each person to attempt to determine the predominate mood or attitude of the writer of the song. What is he trying to say *most of all*? Play the song and allow them time to jot down their opinions. Ask for their conclusions and allow for discussion in so far as several different conclusions will probably emerge.

Next ask them to listen to a reading of the parable of the Prodigal Son (Luke's version). Their task is to listen carefully to determine how many distinct persons are mentioned in the parable. On completion of the reading, ask for results and compare these with the actual number (five). Make appropriate comments about the accuracy/inaccuracy, the difficulty of listening even though we are attentive.

Finally, re-read the parable asking them to listen for the message that Jesus, the teller of the story, wanted most to get across. (He was stressing the narrow-mindedness of the elder son more than the sin of the younger son or the mercy of the Father.) Ask for their conclusions and allow discussion.

Conclude with some comments to the effect that listening is not always easy. It is especially important to learn to listen to what others are really saying. Most importantly, we need to learn *to listen to God, who speaks in many ways*. This kind of listening is one form of prayer. To illustrate, now pass out the apples or whatever natural objects you were able to provide. Tell them to "listen" to it; by touching, looking at, smelling, tasting and in other ways examining it. All the time, they are to ask themselves what is God saying about himself by having created this apple.

Encourage a silent, prayerful attitude during this form of listening and allow them sufficient time to become reflective. Then, ask for reactions with some of the following questions:

1) For you personally, what does God say most loudly by means of the apples he has made?

2) Did you feel foolish "listening" to an apple? How do you feel now? Is it really that foolish?

3) Can you think of any other natural objects that seem to speak loudly about God? What do they say? Do you take much time listening to them?

4) What's really involved in this kind of listening? What are some things that could prevent us from listening in this way, of really being able to hear?

5) Do you think it is safe to describe what we have been doing as one form of prayer? If this is prayer, is it a form of prayer you think is important? One you could learn to enjoy? What kind of results could you expect from this kind of praying?

6) If we truly try to listen to one another, can we say

it is like praying to one another? What would happen to relationships if people learned to "pray" to each other in these ways?

7) Do you think that God can speak to us through people? How real is it to say that by listening to others—parents, friends, teachers, even strangers—we will often be listening to and praying to God?

Conclude this session by asking everyone to listen to a short reading from Scripture. An appropriate one is Mt 19: 16-22. Or choose one more suited to your group. Pause after the reading; then dismiss the group without seeking further comments.

Follow-up

Before concluding the session you may wish to give the following assignment in preparation for the next meeting. Ask the students to spend some time "listening" to God before the next session. Their goal is to try to discern the kinds of ways God uses to speak to us and more importantly, what he may be saying. At the next session begin by asking them to share some of their experiences. Not all will be able to do so, but some will remember enough to provide further opportunity to review the topic.

Do It Yourself Kit

Goal

To help students experience what is involved in prayer which is designed for the person and the group.

Objective

To help them understand and feel at home with this form of praying—personal and communal.

Preparation and Materials

You will want to prepare a copy of the form on the following page for each student. Keep on hand additional copies, extra paper, and pencils.

Note: This form is a suggestion. You may wish to compose another following the same idea but more suited to your group.

Instructions

Divide the students into groups of six to eight. Supply each person with a copy of the form. Tell them that each student is to pick a word from each column that seems most appropriate to him or herself. At the bottom of the paper the student should write out a prayer, using these words. Each student should do *three* such prayers. When this has been done, everyone is to share his or her "prayers" with the rest of the persons in the group. Students need not explain them; it is enough for each student to read his or her "prayers."

Title for God			Title for Self			
Adjective	Noun	Prefix	Adjective	Noun	Verb	Object
Dear	God	your	sinful	servant	needs	help
Heavenly	Father	"	frightened	son	begs for	advice
Gentle	Son	"	confident	daughter	thanks for	forgiveness
Kind	Spirit	"	fearful	child	asks for	you
Forgiving	Creator	"	sorrowful	creature	requests	courage
Loving	Jesus	"	grateful	brother	appreciates	confidence
Just	Christ	"	confused	sister	enjoys	faith
Mysterious	Savior	"	joyful		pleads for	patience
Unseen	Redeemer	"	eager		has	peace
Merciful	Friend	"	angry		deserves	an answer
Powerful	Protector	"	peaceful		searches for	understanding
Faithful	Judge	"	struggling		hopes for	friendship
All wise	Master	"	determined		fears	strength
Patient	Brother	"	lonely		loves	generosity
Trusting	Guide	"	faithful			love

Once this is done, ask each group, using the same form, to develop one group prayer, which seems most appropriate for the entire group.

After that, have each group share its prayer with the other groups. Now each group can explain why and how they arrived at that particular formula, since a group prayer demands less personal revelation from the individual and is thus less threatening. Finally, having shared each group's prayer and the rationale behind it, ask the class as a whole to arrive at one formula that best summarizes the sentiments of the entire class. This should be done as much as possible in a spirit of cooperation, not competition. Encourage as much participation as possible.

The next step is to have the entire class stand in a large circle, holding hands if suitable. Designate one person to begin by saying the class prayer out loud. He then repeats it, this time being joined by the person to his right. The two of them repeat, being joined by the third person and so on, until the whole group is saying the prayer together. Usually a kind of rhythmic cadence is developed.

After all have said the prayer together once or twice, ask them to stop and reassemble for a reaction session, using some of the following questions for starters:

1) In formulating your own personal prayer like this, what are you really doing? Gaining insight into yourself? Gaining insight into God? Do you think this kind of personal prayer is better than ones not made by you? Why?

2) Do you think God answers such prayers? How?

(The answer to the prayer is in a sense contained in the very ability to say it out loud, recognizing who you are and what your relationship to God is at this moment.)

3) How did you feel about the group prayer you composed? The class prayer? Could you identify with it? Completely, partly, not at all? Why? If you could identify with the prayer, can you see any advantage to a group-formulated prayer over your own? Why? Does it help to know others have somewhat the same needs, feelings, concerns, attitudes?

4) How about the prayer in the round? Is there a certain strength in this kind of prayer? Is it because it is louder and God has a better chance to "hear" it, or is it because of the group support and identity involved?

5) Do you see a need for both kinds of prayer—your own private formulas and also those developed by the group? What are the advantages and disadvantages of each?

6) Did you find it helpful to hear other people's ideas and explanations as you tried to formulate a common prayer in your group and then as a whole class? Is this kind of sharing of insights and common understanding, a form of praying? Why? Why not?

7) Can you see any relation between what we have done and other common prayer engaged in by the Church, in particular the Eucharist? Why? Why not?

By now you should have gained some rather good insights into the students' understanding of themselves and of prayer. Your comments or input would largely be determined at this point by what you have discovered, either reinforcing correct notions or challenging and correcting misconceptions.

Follow-up

A most helpful follow-up is to have the class jointly plan and then celebrate a prayer service which is uniquely theirs. Formats would vary but such a service usually includes some songs, readings, petitions, and a collect or summary prayer. Set some time aside for personal reflection. The important dimension here is the process of developing the prayer service. As much as possible it should be a group effort, and it should as much as possible reflect the real sentiments and needs of the entire group. You may want to spend one session in planning and a second in celebrating.

CHAPTER 5

GAMES ON MORAL PROBLEMS

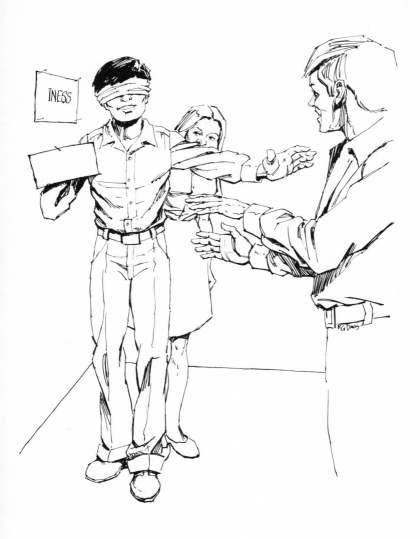

Questionnaire

Goal

To enable students to examine together in a more or less clinical setting certain moral questions.

Objective

To help them discover the questions to be asked in making moral decisions.

Preparation and Materials

Each student will need a copy of the questions presented below and a pencil and paper. The questions could be mimeographed or could be written on a board or overhead.

1) How does this action improve me as an authentic human being?

2) How does it endanger or destroy my humanness?

3) How does this action improve my friends as authentic human beings?

4) How does it endanger or destroy my friends' humanness?

5) How does this action improve my relationship with others: peers, family, society?

6) How does this action endanger or destroy my relationship with others: peers, family, society?

7) How does this action improve my friends' relationship with others: peers, family, society?

8) How does this action endanger or destroy my friends' relationship with others: peers, family, society?

Instructions

This exercise can be applied to most moral problems. In this exercise we will focus on the problem of drinking. At the end of this exercise there are instructions for adapting the material to other problem areas.

Begin by giving each person a copy of the above questions. Explain that the questions reflect the kinds of questions a Christian should ask himself when faced with a moral dilemma. They are the kinds of concerns implied in the commandment of Jesus to love God and to love our neighbor as ourselves. To be authentically Christian is to be authentically human, fully recognizing our dependence on God and our responsibility to love our fellow man as we love ourselves.

After this explanation, pose this problem: You are with a group who is going to stay overnight at a friend's house. The friend's parents will be out of town, and don't know about the party. *Your* parents think adults will be there.

The host points out that there's a large supply of hard liquor on hand. Everyone could get "bombed," sleep it off, and no one's parents would be the wiser.

Each person is now asked to make a decision about getting drunk, using the questionnaire as a basis. That is, he should attempt to answer each question as honestly as he can—alone. Next, form groups of six to eight and ask the group to attempt to arrive at a consensus about the best answer for each question. If this proves impossible, allow each group to present a majority and a minority report to the whole class.

Note: Up to this point the teacher has not been involved in the discussion or in the reporting other than to serve as facilitator and as collector of the final reports. You should feel free to wander in and out of groups, though, observing and helping to clarify the task.

Once you have received all the reports, you are free to observe similarities and differences, ask for further clarification, and seek further reaction from groups about the reports of the others. Your purpose up to this point was to help students learn the right *questions* to ask in dealing with a moral decision. Also, you have provided a relatively safe forum for them to discover what some of their peers are thinking about each problem. In the follow-up you are concerned with sharing the Christian position on the topic.

Follow-up

There is no one formula for the follow-up. Much will depend on how the students answered the questions. If the vast majority seemed to reflect a sound response in terms of the Christian tradition, there isn't much more to be done other than to reinforce that response. The individuals who reject that response can best be approached on an individual basis to discuss it with them further and to counsel them.

If there is a significant group or even a majority who reject the Christian position, the task is to deal with their reasons for justifying the action, testing them out, seeking ways to demonstrate their inaccuracy or incompleteness. This should be done in a calm, non-argumentative way. What must be stressed is the seriousness of action and its consequences for them *and* for others. For that reason, it is critical that their answers be accurate and honest. For *that* reason it is a healthy thing to continue to examine and test them within a classroom or "clinical" setting.

In other words, your approach should not be to "convert" them to your position, but rather to continue to help them think through their own position and its possible consequences.

Alternate uses for this Exercise: The main elements of this exercise can be used for posing many other moral problems that concern students and also for theorizing on certain problems that don't yet affect them. The questions may need to be changed so as to reflect the nature of the act. For example, friends might have to be changed to victims, the one vandalized, the policeman on duty, parents.

In any event the process is the same. Each individual attempts to answer the questions as best he can. These responses are then shared in small groups or pairs and ultimately the whole class attempts to reach some consensus. The teacher then follows up with appropriate sessions based on the student response.

In each instance the teacher should concentrate on helping students clarify *their own* thinking and discovering how *their peers* feel before she or he proposes the Christian position. It is more healthful and more productive for the students to debate with one another than it is to use a structure in which they all join forces to debate with the teacher.

The Wicked Judges

Goal

To give students an experience of what it feels like to be victims of vandalism.

Objective

To initiate discussion into some of the basic issues involved in that form of behavior.

Preparation and Materials

Prior to class, select some of the more popular and self-possessed students. One student for each group of six to eight in your class is necessary. You will want to explain to them the nature of the exercise as described below and ask them to cooperate by being vandals at the appropriate time. Obviously, if anyone refuses, don't demand that he participate, but do ask him not to reveal the activity to others beforehand.

The timing of this activity can help its success. It is best done when the group is engaged in a real project, such as preparing banners for a liturgy. If there is no such opportunity, the initial part of the class must be developed around some project you ask them to do, motivating them in whatever way seems appropriate. For example, you may ask them to divide in groups and have each group attempt to make a symbolic representation of what they think friendship is (or courage, greed, love, sin, school spirit). Provide the necessary materials like poster board, paste, felt pens, old magazines, string, toothpicks, etc.

Instructions

Divide the students into groups and give them instructions for doing the project you have decided. Give the purpose, time limit, how they will be judged, etc. Let them proceed. When all the groups are finished, ask the pre-determined students, one of whom is in each group, to serve as judges. While the judging is to take place, the other students are asked to step out in the corridor, or, if feasible, to take a short refreshment break. In any event all the students except the judges should leave the room, and you should accompany them.

While all are gone, the judges vandalize all the projects in varying degrees from total destruction to only minor alterations. At a prearranged time, return with the students. Observe the reactions and be alert to keep peace. Because the emotional "investment" is little, the anger aroused normally will not be too much to handle. Also, once the initial reaction is over, announce that the vandalism was done intentionally in order to evoke *honest* feelings of reaction.

Assemble the group and initiate discussion with some of the following questions:

1) Everyone seemed angry to some degree. Why were some more angry than others?

2) What were your first feelings toward the obvious vandals? Did you want retaliation? Would you like to see them punished? Were you tempted to do a little "punishing" yourself? What thoughts came across your mind?

3) Did you think the "vandals" were vandal types? Or did you feel surprised at what they did? Did you think

they had some reason for their action? Did you react more in terms of it being a funny joke or a mean thing to do?

4) Since some projects were totally destroyed and others only partially, would the various groups like to compare reactions?

5) Let's suppose that this had not been a put-on but that these students did in fact deliberately vandalize your work just for their own fun? What do you think your reactions would be now? How would you deal with them? What would you want them to do? What would you want to do to them?

6) Have you ever in fact had something like this happen to you in real life? What happened? How did you react? Did you ever find out who did it? If you did, how did you feel toward him? What did you do in return?

7) To the vandals: How did you feel doing it? Why?

8) A certain amount of vandalism seems to happen almost everyday at school, on the way home from school or in the evenings when young people get together. Why? Do you think those vandalized—school personnel, homeowners, shopkeepers, public officials, bus owners, and the like have a right to get angry? If you were such a person vandalized, what would you like to see happen to the vandals, despite their age or good record?

By now you should be able to keep the discussion moving, especially by exploring students' own opinions on why people vandalize, what can be done to prevent it, what kinds of punishment seem appropriate. Ultimately your concern is for them to form some personal decisions about vandalism. Vandalism always hurts somebody and that somebody is a real person.

Follow-up

Ask students to spend some time prior to the next meeting observing some forms of vandalism that have taken place around the school, to some person's property in their neighborhood, to public property like a park. As they do, tell them to try to put themselves in the place of the person vandalized or at least one who must repair the damage: The janitor, for instance, who must repaint a wall or try to remove toilet paper from all the shrubs and trees, the theater owner who must pay someone to repair his broken toilet fixtures, the homeowner who must clean up the mess caused by tipped garbage.

Spend some time during the next meeting discussing their observations and reactions. If possible, move them toward some positive action either for the prevention of vandalism or for repair to vandalized property.

Pin the Tail on Happiness

Goal

To give the students some experience of the feelings involved in the obedience/authority conflict.

Objective

To sensitize them to the real difficulties experienced by their parents and others who must exercise some form of authority over them.

Preparation and Materials

You will need blindfolds, and also straight pins to which are attached slips of paper with the letters: H, A, P, P. Also you will need a piece of poster board taped to a wall, at the center of which are the letters: I, N, E, S, S. The room should be arranged in such a way that there is a clear path from one end of the room to the wall where the poster board is taped.

Instructions

This is a variation of "Pin the Tail on the Donkey." First divide the class into an even number of groups, about six to a group, but they can be larger or smaller for this exercise. Next ask for volunteers, one volunteer for every *two* groups. Explain that the object of the game is for the volunteer, blindfolded, to make a full word by pinning this slip of paper as close to the letters on the poster board as he can. One group of students will assist him in the project by giving him correct instructions. However, another group will hinder him by giving him false instructions. Their object is to get him to walk into any of the four walls. If he touches any of them without having put the slip on the board, he is disqualified. He must figure out, before it is too late, which group is really trying to help him and which is giving him bad advice. Blindfold the volunteer. Ask both groups to come by him, one on each side. Turn the student around several times as in "Pin the Tail" and leave him aimed in any direction. Silently by pointing, designate the group which is to give bad counsel, having explained the signal ahead of time. Indicate that both groups should begin trying to guide the volunteer.

After one volunteer has succeeded or failed, repeat the game with another volunteer and with two new groups. This can be repeated several more times if desirable, changing groups around and using new volunteers. When the exercise has been done at least as often as necessary for everyone to have participated once in some capacity, reassemble the group and initiate discussion with some of the following questions:

1) What were some of your immediate reactions to your experience? (This can be directed independently to "good groups," "bad groups," and volunteers.)

2) To good groups: Can you think of any real life situations where you were trying to help someone but had a lot of flack from others? Like what? What happened? How did you feel when your good advice was rejected?

3) To all: Can you think of situations where you ever felt like the volunteer, that is, you just didn't know where to go or what to do and were getting all kinds of conflicting advice? Like when? What did you do? What finally happened?

4) Do you ever feel that way now? When? Who are some of the conflicting advisors in your life?

5) Granted, it's rough to be in the middle, not being sure who to believe, but how do you think people who are responsible for you feel when they are trying to give you advice and there are all kinds of conflicting advice around for you to follow? Do you think this is how your parents sometimes feel?

6) How right is it for them to think of you as "blindfolded"? Are there times when in fact you really are "blindfolded"? When? In what kinds of situations? In terms of what kinds of decisions? Do you find it hard to listen to your parents at such times? Why? Who do you listen to? With what results?

7) Are there times when parents treat you as if you were blindfolded and in fact you are convinced you can see for yourself? What kinds of situations? How do you react? What's the real solution?

This should provide sufficient grist for more discussion. If and when advisable, you may want to begin to substitute Church or other forms of authority for parents. The same questions and principles will apply.

Follow-up

Ask students to examine and record the number of times their parents give them "bad advice" during the next week—advice meaning anything from telling them they must do their homework before watching TV to refusing to allow them to use the car, to see a particular movie, or to attend a particular party. Or you can use Church or other authority instead. At the end of a week, ask them to report and to explain their conclusions.

Let's Make a Deal

Goal

To give students an experience of the effects of lying in human relations.

Objective

To initiate a discussion on the real significance of lying in the human community.

Preparation and Materials

Divide students into groups of three. For every group you will need two envelopes, each containing a slip of paper on which is written either the number one or the number two. Distribution of numbers is arbitrary. Also each group will have to be supplied with some play money, chips, or other means of counting. About thirty units to a group is adequate.

Instructions

Once the class is divided into groups of three, ask one person from each group to serve as banker. Give each banker twenty chips and have them set up "banks" in various parts of the room. The other persons are all given an envelope and five chips. Each person is playing for himself. The rules of the game are as follows:

1) Each player must take up a position by any banker of his choice.

2) When two players are in front of one banker, they

are to try to sell the contents of their envelope to each other.

3) The object of the game is to gain as many chips as possible in the allotted time.

4) One can gain or lose chips in the following manner:
a) Tell one another the contents of your slip. You may lie, saying you have a one when in fact you have a two.
b) If you accept each other's offer, exchange envelopes.
c) If both in fact lied, both forfeit a chip to the banker.
d) If you accept each other's offer and one person lied, the liar gets one chip from the person fooled.
e) If both told the truth, both receive a chip from the banker.
f) Once the transaction is finished, move on with the new envelope to a new banker and strike another sale.
g) If both do not agree to an exchange, move to another banker and seek another buyer.

5) The banker is to judge who is to give or receive chips. His word is final.

Because these rules are rather complicated, you should take time to explain them carefully and demonstrate a few transactions so all are sure of the rules. Begin the game. After sufficient time has elapsed for all to have made at least a few transactions (it is best to set a time limit so they keep moving), assemble the group and determine who has the most chips. Bankers, of course, are not eligible. Now initiate discussion with some of the following questions:

1) Did anyone discover the trick to the game? If you did, how did you react? Did you share it with others? If not, why not? If so, how did they react?

(*Note:* the trick is simply that if everyone consistently tells the truth everyone consistently collects from the banker. It's the fastest way to gain the most chips. Notice, too, it was never said to gain more chips than others. Simply to gain as many as *you* can in the allotted time.)

2) How did you feel about not being sure if you could trust others?

3) Did you find it challenging to lie? Were you a good liar? If you never tried to lie, why not? What was the effect in chips? Were you tempted to begin to lie?

4) Did you begin to find it hard to trust anyone? How did you feel about it?

5) To bankers: Was there anything you noticed about what was going on you'd like to share?

6) In this game honesty was obviously the best policy — provided everyone is honest. Can honesty ever be the best policy in real life? Why? Why not?

7) Do you think it is fair to say that the real evil in lying is not so much the individual deed but the long-term result of gradually destroying man's confidence in his fellow man to the point where we find it hard to believe anyone? How could we ever arrive at a society where we could rebuild this trust?

8) Would you agree with this statement: Lying is really inhuman because in the long run it makes it impossible for men to relate with each other? Can you think of real situations where you don't trust someone and he or she no longer trusts you? What is it like? What can be done about it?

9) Can one liar in a group make the whole group suspicious of each other? Is this its real harm? Can you think of any real instances of this?

Follow-up

The best follow-up is to play the game again either during the same session or the next one. While everyone now knows the trick of the game the real test will be to see if everyone can trust others enough to always tell the truth. All it would take is for one person to lie one time to start the whole process over. In fact, it might be good to "plant" a liar just for that purpose. Afterwards return to the points suggested by the last few questions about the effect of lying on society.

E. SHOPLIFTING/STEALING

Marketplace

Goal

To give the students an experience of being involved in a suspicion-filled situation.

Objective

To illustrate how stealing in any form infects society with suspicions that make good human relationships difficult if not impossible.

Preparation and Materials

This exercise is a little more elaborate than the preceding ones. You will need one envelope and one slip of paper for each student. On four of the slips write "thief"; on two write "detective"; on all the others write "shopkeeper." Also you will need three chips, or play money of one value, for each of the students. Each student except thieves and detectives is also given a number. This should be indicated on the slip of paper. The room should be arranged so that all desks are placed against the walls facing outward, forming a square. If there are no desks, use tables or chairs. These desks, tables, or chairs will serve as "shops." Each shop is numbered. The student with the corresponding number "owns" that shop. Thieves and detectives do not have shops. In each shop three items should be placed which serve as merchandise. You could use things like gum, candy, apples, pencils. Some variety makes it more interesting.

Instructions

The room should be prearranged as above before students arrive. If possible it is best to give instructions in another room and then bring the students together to the "market." Give each person his envelope containing his title, money, and number. Tell them to show *no one* who he is or what his number is.

The rules are as follows:

1) Four persons have been designated thieves. Their task is to attempt to steal as many items as they can without getting caught. Simply take an item and don't pay for it.

2) Two persons are detectives. Their task is to catch the thieves. If a thief is caught, he is to be sent to the center of the room and to remain there until the end of the game. An arrest is made simply by tapping persons on the shoulder. If you are a thief you must respond.

3) All others are shopkeepers. You are also buyers. Your goal is to sell all your items. But you cannot stay near your own shop all the time. You must move around and buy from other shops.

4) Since no one is minding any of the stores—in fact no one should know who owns what stores—a purchase is made simply by picking up the item of your choice and putting in its place one of your play dollars or chips.

5) If a shopkeeper notices he has been robbed—more items are missing than there are dollars to replace them—he may attempt to steal from another shop to replace his items.

6) Shopkeepers who have sold all their items and have the dollars in exchange are winners. So are the detectives if they catch all four thieves. Thieves are winners if they succeed in stealing three items without getting caught.

Review and demonstrate the rules as necessary so all understand. Begin the exercise after setting an appropriate time limit; about ten minutes is adequate, but you may wish to extend it if there is enough interest. After the time limit, ask shopkeepers to go to their respective shops, take inventory, and report. Uncaught thieves should identify themselves and display their stolen goods if they were successful. Detectives should also identify themselves if their identity hasn't already been discovered. Now assemble the group and initiate discussion with some of the following questions:

1) What was the overall effect of knowing that some in the group were thieves? Did you begin to suspect persons who weren't in fact thieves? Did you find it difficult to go too far from your own shop?

2) How did you feel knowing that even honest shopkeepers could turn thief? Did this make you even more suspicious?

3) Was there any comfort in knowing that some detectives were at work? Would you have preferred to know who they were?

4) If you were a shopkeeper who was robbed, were you tempted to turn thief to recoup your losses? Did you? How did you feel about it? Did you feel justified?

5) To detectives: How did you feel during the game?

Suspicious of everyone? Did you find it hard or easy to detect a thief? Was it frustrating or fun?

6) To the thieves: How did you feel about your assignment? Was it a challenge to try to get away with something? Was it difficult to conceal your identity? How did you feel when relating with "honest" people?

7) Can anyone see what we are really getting at here? Besides the personal property loss for the one robbed, what is the bad effect that stealing has on a group?

8) Can you think of real life situations where you found yourself suspicious of everyone? What was it like?

9) Is there some relationship to stealing and lying? Do both have as their evil the effect of making it impossible for people to relate to each other naturally?

10) If there were no thieves around, what could have happened in the game?

There should have been enough reaction by now for the teacher to begin to discuss the real situation behind things like shoplifting. How do storeowners feel? Are they justified in all the security they employ and in prosecuting thieves? What is it like living in a world like ours where we really can't trust anyone?

Follow-up

A practical follow-up would be to ask a storeowner or security person to talk with students about how shoplifting affects store policy, prices, and the like; and also what happens to a person caught. An alternate or additional follow-up could center around a penance service related to stealing and dishonesty in general.

CHAPTER 6

SUGGESTIONS FOR USING
THE GAMES

Underlying the order in which the games have been arranged is a rationale based upon certain theological presuppositions. Having examined the games, now it should be helpful for you to review those presuppositions and the rationale they suggest.

There is the presupposition in Chapter 1 that a creature is limited and is dependent upon a relationship with God to achieve his ultimate perfection. For man to experience himself as limited can be a discouraging insight (especially if he experiences the depths of his limitations which include sinfulness). It is in the context of that experience that the Good News of Jesus, His promise to mankind, and the Gift of the Spirit can be fully appreciated. Hope is central to the Christian experience and the Christian way of life. To be Christian is to learn how to wait creatively, confidently, and patiently. This is an active waiting, not a passive experience. The proof and the cause of this is the activity of the Spirit in our midst. Thus we are concerned with his role and the role of the prophet in the life of the Christian. The Spirit of Christ is He Who carries out the work of assisting man in his growth toward ultimate perfection. It is critical to man that he learns to recognize the presence and work of this Spirit. It is equally critical that he be sensitive to the absence of that Spirit and be willing to alert others to the dangers inherent to man's destiny whenever the Spirit is resisted.

It is in that context that sin is best understood as man's willful refusal to be what he *knows* he is called to be. If man is called to perfect his humanity through the help of the Spirit, then to sin is to refuse to be human, to become inhuman.

As man grows in humanness it becomes obvious that to be human is to be in community with other men (Chapter 2). Community includes many things: uniqueness and freedom within a framework of mutual cooperation, sharing, supporting, and celebrating to name a few basic dimensions. Given this understanding of humanness, the result of sin would always be to remove oneself—or be removed—from community. This raises the whole question of reconciliation and the process by which a man is reinstated in the community through his sorrow and the community's forgiveness. Within this basic theological framework, prayer (Chapter 3) can be viewed from several angles. Essentially it is presented as the dialogic relationship between God and man. Such dialogue implies the ability to listen, to be sensitive to what the other is saying. There is a close parallel here between prayer and the process involved in discerning the Spirit. Prayer also has a communal or common dimension: the articulation of the community's common experiences, needs, and aspirations. Such common prayer both strengthens the individual and solidifies the community.

Finally, there is the question of the morality of particular actions taken up in Chapter 4. As stated above, to be moral is to become more human, just as to sin is to become inhuman. ("The glory of God is man fully alive.") So the basic test of all moral decisions is the effect the action has on one's growth in humanness. Since this perfection in humanness is viewed in terms of growth in community, immoral or inhuman actions will always have a disruptive influence on community and the individual's ability to relate to others in community. It is in terms of these presuppositions that certain individual moral problems are presented.

The theological framework which underlies the games is not a complete theology but it is sufficiently broad that it can serve as the basis for the introduction of many other theological topics normally treated in any religious education program. For example, it is within the context of the communal nature of man that the nature and mission of the Church can easily be presented. Once a student grasps the concept that a community usually reinstates a rejected member through some ritual celebration of his sorrow and "re-birth," then we can deal with a Sacrament like penance. An understanding of the role of the prophet becomes the most authentic basis for a Christian's involvement in social concerns, even at the risk of personal danger and death.

It should be understood, then, that a definite rationale underlies the development of the games and the order in which they are presented. It should also be understood that these games do not directly embrace every theme and topic essential to religious education. As stated in the introduction, a game is by its nature intended to serve as a lead-in to a particular topic. Once that topic has been broached, however, many other topics begin to suggest themselves, and it won't always be necessary to play another game to arouse students' interest in pursuing them. The games, taken in sequence, could conceivably be used as a full course for a given year or given program. This would presuppose, though, that the teacher does more than play these games. Once the topic is introduced he should help students pursue it by means of his full arsenal of proven teaching techniques: films on the topic, speakers, discussions, research projects, service projects, field trips, readings—whatever seems necessary.

While the order of the presentation of the games does have a certain inner logic that could move the student from point A to B in a progressive series of insights and experiences, there are several other ways the games can be used.

First, they could be presented individually as they fit the curriculum you are using. For example, if the year is being spent primarily on sacraments, the game on reconciliation might be used at an appropriate time with the sacrament of penance without using the games that precede or follow it. In other words, if a game seems to offer one possibility for presenting a topic you are committed to teach, use it on its own merits.

Second, one group of games could be used as the basis for developing a unit or theme without reference to the other games. The series on the Spirit could form the nucleus for a unit on the Spirit in preparation for confirmation. The series on prayer could serve as the basis for a unit on prayer. The same could be said for the series on moral problems in relation to a unit on morality.

Another alternative suggests itself—a kind of mix-and-match approach. The game on the nature of sin could be used in conjunction with the game on reconciliation as the basis for preparing students for a penance service or for the celebration of the sacrament of reconciliation.

Finally in schools and parishes where retreat evenings, overnights, or weekends are an integral part of the religious program, a combination of several of these games could be used as introductions to the topics to be covered. Games are especially suited for these more leisurely situations. You can have a game followed by some discussion and then a more formal presentation to tie things together. With three or four "units," separated by meals and social events, you have a rather complete weekend program. For example, I've seen a very effective overnight built around the "Waiting Game" as the starter around 8:00 the first evening. The game finishes with a party which is a good way to close the first evening.

This was followed in the morning with the "Senses Walk," discussion, and a formal presentation on the nature of community. Lunch and a rest break follow. The "Reconciliation Game," discussion, penance service and Agape Supper which included a Eucharistic celebration. Back home by 7:00 p.m., twenty-four hours later. Remember, the key to this program was not the games. They served as stimulators or pivots. The real guts of the program revolved around the leadership, the formal presentations, and the liturgy—as any good program would.

So games aren't a panacea, but they do often make planning and executing a class or program easier, if not always simpler. If you are comfortable with the underlying theological presuppositions of the games presented and if you appreciate the limitations all games contain, I'm confident you will find these games helpful to you in your work in religious education. More important, I'm confident you'll be stimulated to begin developing your own—and better—games for future use.

TIPS FOR
EFFECTIVE DISCUSSION

Several principles must be observed if discussion as a catechetical technique is to be effective. The purpose of this appendix is to present and analyze these principles. Such principles can be organized into the following categories:

1) General Principles
2) Principles Related to Motivation
3) Principles Related to Structuring the Discussion Proper
4) Principles Related to Summary/Teacher Participation

1) General Principles

a) Discussion is a form of dialogue useful for helping participants reflect upon matters of importance to them and for facilitating their decisions regarding the effect these matters should have on their lives.

As such, discussion as a method must be situated in a larger learning process. It is one step. Preceding it must be some form of experience or awakening requiring reflection on the part of the students. Following it comes the process of decision-making and the integration of the new insights into one's life style. The implication is, "Don't ask discussion to do what it can't." As an activity isolated from the larger learning process, most discussion is a meaningless exercise and students will react accordingly.

b) Discussion as a means of reflection implies a psychological readiness for reflection "in dialogue." This kind of readiness normally won't be found in students below the junior high level. As a regular method for facilitating reflection it is not effective until about the junior year (age 16) and beyond. (Note, we stress the word "regular.")

The importance of this principle can't be sounded too often. As a method of education, discussion is rather sophisticated and calls for a degree of sophistication on the part of the students. "Talking," "sharing ignorance," "mouthing platitudes" is not discussion. When a planned discussion takes such a form one of two things is wrong. Proper motivation is lacking (we will deal with that shortly), or students are simply too young to be expected to carry on a meaningful discussion.

c) For effective discussion, the size of the group should normally be not less than six and no greater than twelve. Eight is usually considered an optimum number.

This principle is self-explanatory, but it might be helpful to make one observation: If the topic is "hot," keep the groups small so everyone can say his piece; if it is more subdued, a larger group will insure a greater variety of input and consequent stimulation. Keeping these basic principles in mind we can proceed to those governing the critical question of motivation.

2) Motivation

a) Students will be naturally motivated to discuss an experience that has potential meaning for themselves or which contradicts their previous experience.

This principle could be very complex. In view of the

fact that most readers are interested in practical rather than theoretical information, I'll limit myself to a practical kind of commentary. The key point is that discussion is natural if a shared experience "moved" the participants. A homely example: conversation at a cocktail party after a football game. Small groups form and "discuss the game." They are bound together by a common experience and each person wants to share his interpretation as to why the game ended the way it did. The topic isn't particularly salvific, but it illustrates the point. People will discuss—and gain insights—whenever something excites them. The implication for catechists, in terms of motivating a discussion, is that discussion will "work" whenever the students have shared an experience significant to them. Providing and/or recognizing such experiences is the best form of motivating meaningful discussion. A kind of corollary is that discussion should follow as soon as possible after the experience (e.g. at a party a week after a football game, the discussion will not naturally evolve around the game).

b) In the absence of such providential or programmed experiences, motivation for discussion must rest upon experiences typical to the student group.

This principle can best be explained by pro and contra examples. Pro: Sophomore students normally experience a certain strain in relating to parents over the question of personal autonomy. Contra: Sophomores normally don't have any personal investment in the question of conscientious objection. The conclusion: A certain natural motivation is present if the teacher suggests discussion on the topic of parental authority, but only a theoretical concern for the question of conscientious objection. I assume the point is made regarding typical experiences and the consequent motivation to discuss.

c) Typical experiences must be translated into concrete goals and, if possible, action goals in order to motivate meaningful discussion.

This is at the heart of most discussion situations promoted by religion teachers. Examples may help clarify the full implications of the principle. First a concrete goal: "Can you decide as a group upon the three most 'unfair' rules your parents set for you as young adults?" An action goal: "Try as a group to decide the 'one' thing you think you can do effectively to convince your parents you are no longer children." The topic is typical of adolescent experience. A concrete goal demands specifics as an aid to clarification of the real meaning of ongoing experience. An action goal demands specific suggestions as to what can be done regarding a typical experience.

In either case, motivation to discuss depends on translating a typical experience into a very concrete problem with which students not only can grapple but want to grapple. Note, there is no mention of "discuss" which suggests theory or safe abstractions. In each case the participants are challenged to achieve a concrete goal they are typically interested in reaching. The alert teacher never says, "Let's discuss . . ." He/she always says, "Try to decide . . ." or "Can you come up with . . ."

In summary, the key to motivation and, consequently, to the ultimate effectiveness of the discussion method of reflection, depends on unique experiences common to the group or on typical experiences translated into concrete goals for discussing. If the teacher respects the general principles mentioned above and motivates discussion in one of the suggested ways, the rest is just mechanics.

3) Structuring Discussion

a) Once you have announced the goal (motivated discussion), set a time limit, and be stingy in setting it.

Time limits psychologically (especially considering our task-oriented society) and creates a sense of urgency and direction. Being stingy is just good sense. If you think the group can achieve the goal in forty minutes, give them thirty. Let them ask for more time. Nothing is more satisfying to the teacher than hearing students say, "We need more time." Nothing is more secure than knowing you have already planned how to fill the last ten minutes if students don't ask for more time.

b) Set a few ground rules to be used in arriving at the goal.

Note: the ground rules are intended to insure arriving at the goal. They govern any good discussion, but don't present them as such. I have in mind some of the following:

If there are eight in the group, you have a right to talk 1/8th of the time, unless the group wants to hear more from you.

Never interrupt; never ridicule another's ideas or comments; always attempt to hear why a person says what he says. (This latter point suggests some observations about the affective content of any group process. Adapt this to the maturity of the group.)

Interpret silence as concern, not disinterest. (This is a good rule for teachers too, since quiet members might be involved in reflection and dialogue more than vocal members. Listening is one half the dialogue!)

Other ground rules can be presented in keeping with the group and situation. Just remember that their purpose is to facilitate discussion, not motivate it.

c) In mixed groups that are less mature it is a good rule to seat persons "boy-girl, boy-girl."

This arrangement capitalizes on natural needs to "perform" in the presence of the opposite sex and minimizes the security-based tete-a-tetes between participants of the same sex.

d) As much as possible, provide a working environment of tables, hard chairs, paper, pencils, newsprint, and marking pencils, etc.

This principle may seem to contradict the informal nature of a good discussion. However, soft chairs, lying around on floors, casual clusters of friends, soft drinks and pizza, only work in situations where the participants are already highly motivated to discuss, due to a recent, highly significant experience. In more academic, typically motivated discussions, a sense of task enhanced by a working environment is much more effective. Getting people physically close around a table — goal stated, pencils ready — is a great aid to stimulating good discussion.

4) Summary, Teacher Participation

a) About five minutes before the time limit, ask the group(s) to appoint a sceretary-reporter to present the group's conclusion.

This is both a practical principle and a safety valve. The teacher needs a report, as will be seen shortly. A "warning" that the group must make a report in five minutes forces it to come up with something, and, in my experience, this panic report is usually very reflective of the tenor of the discussion to that point. Appointing a secretary or reporter at the beginning usually insures a report, but an artificial one. If no one knows until the very end who has to report, alertness is stimulated and the report is more likely to be spontaneous and objective.

b) The teacher begins to participate directly when student discussion ends.

To this point, of course, the teacher has been very involved in an indirect way. Recognizing or stimulating motivation, formulating the goal, structuring the overall process—these are all tasks of the "discussion leader." If he does these well, however, he is not needed during the discussion. Motivation, concrete goal, time limit, report—these insure that something will happen. The teacher enters after it has happened. Now he is free to react to the reports precisely as a free agent. He can challenge, praise, corroborate, improve upon, provoke further reflection as an independent. He may have been out of the room, certainly out of the group when it arrived at its decision. It is the group's decision and each individual in the group feels a certain security in that fact. Teacher remarks can be listened to and reacted to by students objectively because the teacher is reacting to the group's decisions.

In short, if discussion is properly motivated and structured, the teacher has fulfilled his basic task—facilitating reflection on the topic. What he can add to that reflection by way of personal comment, reference to other experts (e.g., Church authority), inadequacies in the group's decision and the like, can be heard by the individuals in the group precisely because they are members of a group. No individual needs to be embarrassed by honest teacher reactions. Consequently, each individual is open to hear these reactions. That's the beauty and major function of group discussion as a catechetical method: It can create an objectivity and openness that other methods can't.

Conclusion

Properly planned, discussion is one of the most effective methods available to catechists—occasionally in junior high school, regularly in senior high school. Its success will depend upon motivation that "happens," is programmed, or stimulated by presenting concrete goals related to typical experiences of the group. Structure it in terms of size, seating, setting time, report, teacher reaction. And wait for them to ask for more opportunities.